Potions and Herbology at Hogwarts

A Yummy Take on Our Favorite Hogwarts Classes

by

Meg Blair

Copyright © 2021 Meg Blair. All rights reserved.

Copyright Notes

No part of this Book can be reproduced in any form or by any means including print, electronic, scanning or photocopying unless prior permission is granted by the author.

All ideas, suggestions and guidelines mentioned here are written for informative purposes. While the author has taken every possible step to ensure accuracy, all readers are advised to follow information at their own risk. The author cannot be held responsible for personal and/or commercial damages in case of misinterpreting and misunderstanding any part of this Book

Table of Contents

Introduction 5

    Recipe 1: Yorkshire Pudding 7

    Recipe 2: Knickerbocker Glory 9

    Recipe 3: Chocolate Frogs 11

    Recipe 4: Treacle Tart 13

    Recipe 5: Roast Beef and Boiled Potatoes 16

    Recipe 6: Harry's Sticky Chocolate Birthday Cake 19

    Recipe 7: Tasty Bacon Sandwich with Love 23

    Recipe 8: Sweet Berry Trifle 25

    Recipe 9: English Breakfast Delight 28

    Recipe 10: Aunt Petunia's Pudding Masterpiece 31

    Recipe 11: Soft and Chewy Treacle Fudge 33

    Recipe 12: Iced Pumpkin Juice 35

    Recipe 13: Butterbeer 37

    Recipe 14: Melts-in-the-Mouth Choco Pudding 39

    Recipe 15: Quick and Easy Cheesy Baked Salmon 42

    Recipe 16: Pretty Crisp Crumpets 44

Recipe 17: Cauldron Cakes 46

Recipe 18: Beauxbatons' Favorite Bouillabaisse 49

Recipe 19: Sausage Scramble 53

Recipe 20: Holiday Pork Goulash 55

Recipe 21: Hagrid's No-Fail Beef Casserole 57

Recipe 22: Pale Blancmange 60

Recipe 23: Delightful Breakfast Toast 62

Recipe 24: Steak and Kidney Pie 64

Recipe 25: Pumpkin Pasties 67

Recipe 26: English Porridge 69

Recipe 27: Slughorn's Crystallized Pineapples 71

Recipe 28: Roast Chicken Legs and Chips 73

Recipe 29: Hagrid's Rock Cakes 75

Recipe 30: Wild Mushrooms Dinner 77

Recipe 31: Kreacher's French Onion Soup 79

Recipe 32: Cheesy Garlic Pull Apart Bread 81

Recipe 33: Artichoke Canapés 83

Author's Afterthoughts 85

Introduction

With potions and herbology being our two favorite classes at Hogwarts, we thought it was time to put all the stirring and chopping to some good use in the kitchen. While we love magic, food can also be magical when it's delicious, so we thought we'd give some recipes a try since we're already so good at stirring things! Thus, we've put together this cookbook together with the help of all your favorite Hogwarts teachers and classmates.

Each chapter of the book has been inspired by a book, so get ready to find meals and treats inspired by the potions and herbology classes at Hogwarts each year! We've got roast beef with boiled potatoes, treacle tart, bacon sandwiches, trifle, pumpkin juice, chauldron cakes, goulash, onion soup, and lots more! The only question now is, did you participate enough in class to have built up a muscle from all the stirring and chopping? We're going to be needing those skills like never before!

If, for whatever reason, you were dozing off in the back of the classroom during class, just make sure to hit the gym every now and then because you can't wing these recipes like you winged the classes...Either way, we're excited to see you get started! What are you craving today? Pick well and Harry may just join you at home for dinner! Good luck!

HHHHHHHHHHHHHHHHHHHHHHHHHHHHHHHHHHH

Recipe 1: Yorkshire Pudding

Harry's first experience with the grand Hogwarts start-of-term feast made his mouth fall open. He had never seen so many of the things that he likes to eat in one neat pile on the dining table. One of the most memorable dishes is Yorkshire Pudding which is regular fare in British dinners that is often served with roast beef, lamb chops, and other savory dishes.

Portion Size: 4

Prep Time: 55 minutes

Ingredient List:

- ½ lb. flour
- 2 eggs
- 17 oz. cream
- ¼ tsp. salt
- 2 tbsp. meat drippings

HHHHHHHHHHHHHHHHHHHHHHHHHHHHHHHHHHHHHH

How to Cook:

1. Preheat oven to 425 °F.

2. Mix the flour and salt in a bowl. Put a hole in the center, break the eggs into the hole. Stir continuously to mix.

3. Add the cream gradually, stirring until well combined. Set aside.

4. Grease the muffin tins with the meat drippings. Place in the oven for 5-10 minutes, until the dripping smokes.

5. Scoop batter into the muffin tins till they're ¾ full. Let it rest for 2-3 minutes.

6. Reduce temperature to 375 °F, bake the pudding for 15 minutes or until lightly browned.

Recipe 2: Knickerbocker Glory

It was Dudley's birthday, over 10 years since Harry had been left to the care of his Aunt Petunia and Uncle Vernon, when Harry had one of the best days because he was handed this treat. It does not matter if it was given to him because Dudley threw a tantrum, complaining that it was not big enough. What matters is that Harry had a taste of this heavenly dessert, featuring layers of different ice cream variants, fresh strawberries, nuts, and topped with whipped cream.

Portion Size: 4

Prep Time: 30 minutes

Ingredient List:

- 4 scoops strawberry ice cream
- 4 scoops vanilla ice cream
- 1 cup sliced fresh strawberries
- ½ cup dry roasted almonds
- ½ cup dry roasted cashews
- Whipped cream

For Strawberry Compote:

- 2 ½ cups fresh strawberries, sliced
- ½ cup sugar
- 2 tbsp. water
- ½ tsp. lemon juice

HHHHHHHHHHHHHHHHHHHHHHHHHHHHHHHHHHHH

How to Cook:

1. To prepare the strawberry compote, mix the sliced strawberries, sugar, lemon juice, and water until the sugar is dissolved.

2. Cook over low heat until the sauce thickens or for about 20 minutes. Set aside to cool.

3. To assemble, lay fresh strawberries at the bottom of a tall sundae glass. Add one scoop of vanilla ice cream, one scoop of strawberry ice cream, and one scoop of strawberry compote. Stir in some nuts.

4. Top with the whipped cream and sprinkle more nuts on top before serving.

Recipe 3: Chocolate Frogs

It was Harry's first taste of candy bars, wizard-style. He shared his packets of Chocolate Frogs with Ron and, after confirming they are not really frogs, ate it all the while impressed that each comes with a collectible card revealing famous witches and wizards. Apart from chocolate frogs, Harry bought several other treats from the trolley on their way to Hogwarts, such as Bertie Bott's Every-Flavour Beans, Liquorice Wands, Drooble's Best Blowing Gum, Cauldron Cakes, and Pumpkin Pasties.

Portion Size: 10

Prep Time: 55 minutes

Ingredient List:

- 8 Tbsp. gelatin powder
- 2 1/4 cups milk, divided
- 2 cups cocoa powder
- ¾ cup sugar
- Dash of salt
- 2 tsp. vanilla

HHHHHHHHHHHHHHHHHHHHHHHHHHHHHHHHHHHH

How to Cook:

1. Mix gelatin and 1/3 cup milk in a bowl until the powder is dissolved. Set aside.

2. Heat the remaining milk together with sugar, cocoa powder, and salt in a medium saucepan over medium heat. Stir frequently until everything is completely dissolved and the mixture starts to bubble.

3. Turn off heat.

4. Add the gelatin mixture and vanilla.

5. Allow the mixture to cool a little (roughly 5 minutes) before pouring it into molds.

6. Freeze the chocolate frogs for 20-30 minutes to allow them to firm up.

Recipe 4: Treacle Tart

Another grand feast staple, which Harry first tasted on the start-of-term feast, is this delightful yet very simple dessert. It turned out to be Harry's favorite during this meal and into the future. Why not? This tart is made special by golden syrup and sticky molasses. It is not very sweet, but it is truly delightful.

Portion Size: 6

Prep Time: 190 minutes

Ingredient List:

For the Pastry:

- 2 ½ cups all-purpose flour
- 10 oz. cold butter, cubed
- 2 tbsp. sugar
- 1 tsp. salt
- 6 tbsp. cold water

For the Filling:

- 1 cup golden syrup
- Juice and zest of 1 lemon
- 2 ½ cups fresh breadcrumbs
- 1 egg combined with 1 Tbsp. water to brush over the pastry

HHHHHHHHHHHHHHHHHHHHHHHHHHHHHHHHHHHH

How to Cook:

1. Combine 2/3 of the flour with sugar and salt in a mixing bowl.

2. Stir in the butter cubes until the mixture starts to clump.

3. Add remaining flour, mixing until the dough is crumbly.

4. Fold in cold water to bring the dough together.

5. Cut the dough in half, placing each half in a plastic wrap.

6. Place in the fridge for two hours or overnight.

7. Before working the dough, preheat oven to 400 °F.

8. On a lightly floured surface, roll one-half of the dough to cover a 9-inch pie dish. Use the other half to make the lattice topping.

9. For the filling, heat golden syrup in a saucepan over low fire until runny.

10. Crumble breadcrumbs in the food processor. Transfer into a bowl. Add golden syrup, lemon zest, and lemon juice. Mix well.

11. Pour the filling into the prepared dish with the dough, top with the lattice topping, then brush with the egg wash.

12. Bake until the crust becomes golden brown, about 10 minutes.

Recipe 5: Roast Beef and Boiled Potatoes

Much like every mealtime since Harry was introduced to the wizarding world, the Christmas feast at Hogwarts is nothing short of grand and delicious. There were countless dishes laid out on the table for the students who stayed behind to savor. Although the school is not as packed as usual since others took a holiday at home, both Harry and Ron enjoyed Christmas, Hogwarts style. Apart from about a hundred roast turkeys, there were also chipolatas, buttered peas, and mountains of roast beef and boiled potatoes. That's what we are featuring in this section. Try this recipe at home and you will surely feel like the Holidays came early.

Portion Size: 4

Prep Time: 80 minutes

Ingredient List:

- 2 lbs. beef, top rump joint
- 1 tsp. flour
- ½ tsp. mustard powder
- 1 onion, cut into wedges
- 1 lb. small potatoes, skin on
- 1 head garlic, halved
- 1 pc bay leaf
- 1 tsp. peppercorns
- 4 tbsp. unsalted butter
- 1 Tbsp. parsley, chopped
- Salt and pepper to taste

For the Gravy:

- 1 Tbsp. flour
- 1 ½ cups beef stock

HHHHHHHHHHHHHHHHHHHHHHHHHHHHHHHHHHHH

How to Cook:

1. Preheat oven to 400 °F.

2. Whisk mustard powder and flour in a bowl. Rub generously onto beef.

3. Prepare a roasting pan, placing onion wedges at the bottom to serve as the beef's bed.

4. Arrange beef and roast at high temp for 20 minutes. Reduce heat to 325 degrees F, cooking beef for 30-60 minutes, depending on your preferred doneness.

5. While the beef is roasting, boil potatoes in a saucepan over medium-high heat in water together with the bay leaf, garlic, and peppercorns. Season with salt and pepper.

6. Once the potatoes start to boil, reduce the heat to low, and simmer until the potatoes are fork tender or for about 8-10 minutes.

7. Drain potatoes, discarding the peppercorns, bay leaf, and garlic. Then, toss in butter, salt, pepper, and chopped parsley. Set aside.

8. When roast beef is done, transfer it onto a serving plate (reserve meat drippings), cover with foil, and set aside. You need to rest beef but keep it warm for about half an hour prior to serving.

9. While waiting, heat meat drippings in a saucepan. Whisk in flour, stirring continuously until lump-free. Gradually add the beef stock and simmer until sauce thickens a bit.

10. Serve roast beef with boiled potatoes and gravy.

Recipe 6: Harry's Sticky Chocolate Birthday Cake

The day before Harry's 11th birthday, his uncle decided to leave home, fleeing from the letters that were assaulting their house. It was the dreaded Hogwarts letter which Hagrid would bring personally to their hiding place in the middle of an enraged sea. Along with his news about Harry being wizard, he also brought a sticky chocolate cake, similar to this one, as a present to celebrate the young boy's birthday. It was memorable not for its green icing but primarily for the fact that it was the first time Harry's birthday was ever recognized.

Portion Size: 12

Prep Time: 75 minutes

Ingredient List:

- 1 ¾ cups all-purpose flour
- ¾ cup cocoa powder, unsweetened
- 2 cups granulated sugar
- ¾ tsp. salt
- 1 ½ tsp. baking soda
- 2 eggs
- ½ cup butter
- 1 cup buttermilk
- 1 Tbsp. vanilla extract
- 2 tsp. instant coffee dissolved in 1 cup of boiling water
- Cooking spray

For the Chocolate Filling:

- ¾ cup butter at room temperature
- 5 1/3 cups sugar
- 1 ½ cups cocoa powder
- 2/3 cup milk
- 1 tsp. vanilla extract

For the Frosting:

- 6 tbsp. butter at room temperature
- 5 ½ cups sugar
- 1/3 cup milk
- 1 tsp. vanilla extract
- Red and green food coloring

HHHHHHHHHHHHHHHHHHHHHHHHHHHHHHHHHHHHH

How to Cook:

1. Preheat oven to 350 °F. Prepare 2 9-inch cake pans by greasing them with cooking spray. Set aside.

2. Combine the flour, cocoa powder, sugar, salt, and baking soda in a mixing bowl.

3. Add the eggs one at a time, then the butter, buttermilk, and vanilla extract. Mix until smooth.

4. Stir in the prepared hot coffee, mixing until runny using a rubber spatula.

5. Evenly divide the batter in to two prepared pans and then bake for 35 minutes or until a toothpick inserted has come out clean.

6. Cool the cakes on a wire rack before assembling.

7. For the chocolate filling, mix together cocoa powder and sugar in a bowl. Cream butter until it becomes fluffy, then, add 1/3 of the cocoa and sugar mixture plus 1/3 of the milk, beating continuously. Repeat until all the ingredients for the filling, including vanilla extract, are combined and the mixture is spreadable.

8. For the frosting, cream the butter, adding ½ each of sugar and milk alternately. Repeat with the remaining half. Stir in the vanilla extract before dividing the mixture into two bowls, coloring one with green food color and another with a bit of red food color to create pink frosting.

9. Spoon the chocolate filling on top of the first cake layer, smoothing it out as you go. Place the second cake layer on top, firmly pressing down to sandwich the filling.

10. Coat the cake with pink frosting. Do not be careful when smoothing out. The rowdier the top frosting is, the more it will look like the one that Hagrid brought.

11. Finally, place the green frosting in a piping bag, cut the tip, and write, "Happee Birthdae Harry." Don't worry if it is misspelled. It was from Hagrid, after all.

Recipe 7: Tasty Bacon Sandwich with Love

When it's from Mrs. Molly Weasley even simple recipes taste grand because each is made with love. Prior to their trip to Diagon Alley to buy school things for Hogwarts, the kind matriarch stuffed them all with half a dozen bacon sandwiches. We imagine the sandwich is quite delightful if Harry and the rest downed that many in one sitting.

Portion Size: 2

Prep Time: 10 Minutes

Ingredient List:

- 4 pcs cooked bacon
- 4 pcs tomato slices
- 4 pcs cheese slices
- 4 pcs white bread
- 4 tbsp. butter, softened

HHHHHHHHHHHHHHHHHHHHHHHHHHHHHHHHHHHH

How to Cook:

1. Butter each piece of bread generously.

2. Preheat a skillet or flat grill over low heat. Grease the pan with about a tbsp. of butter.

3. Place buttered bread onto the skillet.

4. Top two of the bread slices with 1 cheese slice, 2 bacon strips, 2 tomato slices, and another slice of cheese.

5. Cover each with the remaining bread slices.

6. Keep cooking the sandwich, turning once until both bread sides are browned. Serve.

Recipe 8: Sweet Berry Trifle

This recipe is one of the dishes served during the last memorable feast of the term. It was memorable not only because it was almost the end of the term but because of the trouble related to the opening of the Chamber of Secrets was over and done. The all-night party also hailed Hagrid's homecoming from Azkaban, Gryffindor's win for the House Cup the second year in a row, and the exam cancellations. All of which made everyone hungry for the sweet treat of trifle. Intrigued about how it actually tastes? We know you are! We prepared an easy-to-make berry trifle recipe below.

Portion Size: 8

Prep Time: 25 Minutes

Ingredient List:

- 1 7-oz package Lady Fingers
- 1 qt strawberries, sliced into ¼-inch thick pieces
- 12 oz. blueberries
- 12 oz. raspberries
- 8 oz. raspberry jam
- 1 ¾ cups Confectioner's sugar
- 1 ½ cups heavy cream, chilled
- 16 oz. cream cheese, stored at room temperature
- 1 tsp. vanilla

For Garnish:

- Mint spring

HHHHHHHHHHHHHHHHHHHHHHHHHHHHHHHHHHHH

How to Cook:

1. Place raspberry jam in the microwave for about a minute or until it becomes liquidy.

2. Toss in the fresh berries, saving some for garnish. Coat them completely. Set aside.

3. Beat heavy cream until it forms stiff peaks. Set aside in a bowl.

4. Gradually beat softened cream cheese by adding one third of the sugar, mixing until smooth, then adding the next third, and the next. Continue beating until well combined.

5. Arrange crisp Lady Fingers at the bottom of a glass dish, top with 1/3 of the berry mixture, 1/3 of the heavy cream, and 1/3 of the cream cheese. Repeat the layers until all the ingredients are assembled.

6. Garnish with the remaining fresh berries and fresh mint sprig.

7. This is best when served after chilling for 8 hours or overnight.

Recipe 9: English Breakfast Delight

Since Harry and Ron missed the welcome feast and were only given a plate of sandwiches and a jug of iced pumpkin juice, they could not wait for breakfast. They were not disappointed. Laid neatly on all of the house tables were the elements of a full English breakfast. If you aren't British, then you might be quite curious about what this breakfast is about. That's why we included this recipe – an elaborate and simply mouthwatering English Breakfast Delight, with kippers, bacon, sausages, baked beans, and more.

Portion Size: 4

Prep Time: 45 Minutes

Ingredient List:

- 8 pcs eggs
- 2 cans Kipper, flaked
- 8 pcs breakfast sausages
- 4 slices bacon
- 2 cans baked beans
- 1/3 lb. Black Pudding, sliced
- 1 lb. mushrooms, cleaned and trimmed
- 8 slices white bread
- 4 tbsp. butter, softened
- 2 pcs tomatoes, sliced
- 1 clove garlic, minced
- 2 tbsp. chives, chopped
- Salt and Pepper to taste

HHHHHHHHHHHHHHHHHHHHHHHHHHHHHHHHHH

How to Cook:

1. Heat a large pan over medium-low heat. Cook sausages until brown on all sides or for about 15-20 minutes.

2. In another pan, crisp the bacon over medium-high heat. This should take about 10 minutes or more, depending on the level of crispiness that you prefer.

3. Meanwhile, sauté mushrooms and garlic with a tbsp. of butter. Set aside.

4. Use the same pan in cooking black pudding until crisp. You may grease the pan further with butter if you need to. Set aside.

5. Cook the eggs according to your liking (poached, sunny-side-up, or scrambled). Set aside.

6. Butter the bread slices and toast until slightly brown and crisp. Place the cooked egg on top.

7. Brown the tomato slices in a bit of butter. Set aside.

8. Warm kippers in the same pan. Place on top of buttered toast with the egg.

9. Heat the baked beans for about 3 minutes.

10. To assemble, place a set of two sausages, one bacon slice, a tbsp. of sautéed mushroom and garlic, two slices of black pudding, toast with eggs and kipper flakes, and a tbsp. of baked beans. Enjoy a hearty start-of-day meal.

Recipe 10: Aunt Petunia's Pudding Masterpiece

Nobody knew how this actually tasted since Dobby made it crash onto the floor to foil Harry's return to Hogwarts. What we all know is that it looked mouthwatering and grand with a huge mound of whipped cream and decorative sugared violets for the topping. Try this recipe as it may be the closest you could get to Aunt Petunia's masterpiece of a pudding.

Portion Size: 8

Prep Time: 50 minutes

Ingredient List:

- 1 ¼ cups Oreo baking crumbs
- 1 pack instant pudding
- ¼ cup margarine
- 1 ½ cups milk
- 1 ½ cups whipping cream

For the Sugared Violets:

- 20 pcs violet flowers with 2 inches of stem
- 2 tbsp. powdered sugar
- 1 egg white

HHHHHHHHHHHHHHHHHHHHHHHHHHHHHHHHHHHHHH

How to Cook:

1. Combine the Oreo crumbs and margarine. Press onto the bottom of a 9-inch pie pan. Set aside.

2. Beat milk and pudding mix until smooth. Stir in half of whipping cream, mixing until well combined.

3. Spoon the pudding mixture into a prepared pan.

4. Place in the fridge until it is firm or about 20 minutes.

5. Meanwhile, make the sugared violets by beating the egg white until frothy. Set aside in a bowl.

6. Dip the violets into the egg whites, then sprinkle powdered sugar on top.

7. Arrange the sugared violets on a paper towel lined dish. Place in the refrigerator until the petals have absorbed much of the egg white and sugar, creating a beautiful glaze.

8. To assemble, top the pudding with the remaining whipped cream. Decorate with sugared violets.

Recipe 11: Soft and Chewy Treacle Fudge

Hagrid is not a very good source of treats. They certainly doubted his ability to offer anything edible even if it sounded like it could be delicious. For Christmas, Harry received Treacle Fudge from the friendly giant. Harry ate it and it wasn't bad. Only, it needed softening by the fire before it was consumed. In this recipe, we promise not to give you the same problem. You can well eat it as is.

Portion Size: 6

Prep Time: 40 Minutes

Ingredient List:

- 2 tbsp. treacle or golden syrup
- ½ cup unsalted butter
- 1 cup white sugar
- 1 cup brown sugar
- ½ cup heavy cream
- 1 tsp. vanilla
- ¼ tsp. cream of tartar

HHHHHHHHHHHHHHHHHHHHHHHHHHHHHHHHHHHHHH

How to Cook:

1. Grease an 8-inch serving dish with a bit of butter. Set aside.

2. Whisk in the treacle, the remaining butter, white sugar, brown sugar, heavy cream, and cream of tartar in a saucepan. Heat over medium heat, stirring frequently until the ingredients are well combined and the butter has completely melted.

3. Stop stirring but continue to cook the mixture until its temperature reaches 240 °F on a candy thermometer.

4. Remove from the heat before adding vanilla. Then, set aside to cool a bit.

5. Beat mixture for about 15 minutes until its consistency is similar to peanut butter.

6. Transfer to the prepared, lightly greased dish. Make sure it is evenly spread.

7. Cover with plastic wrap while it cools completely and hardens.

8. Cut into squares before serving.

Recipe 12: Iced Pumpkin Juice

Most of the other characters in the series are fond of downing flagons of pumpkin juice. During the last part of the term, prior to Professor Trelawney's prediction about the Dark Lord coming back with the help of his ever most faithful servant, Harry, Ron, and Hermione are found lounging at the ground with iced pumpkin juice in hand. They were contemplating the exams after the euphoria over Gryffindor's win of the Quidditch Cup finally wear off. Are you curious about how delicious, refreshing, and healthy that might be? No need to just wonder because we have the recipe here for you.

Portion Size: 4

Prep Time: 10 Minutes

Ingredient List:

- ½ cup puréed pumpkin
- 1 cup apple juice
- ½ cup pineapple juice
- ½ cup vanilla yogurt
- 1 Tbsp. honey
- 6 cups ice

For Garnish:

- Whipped cream
- Cinnamon sugar

HHHHHHHHHHHHHHHHHHHHHHHHHHHHHHHHHHH

How to Cook:

1. Combine all the ingredients for the juice in a blender, blending until smooth.

2. Divide equally into glasses.

3. Top with whipped cream and sprinkle with cinnamon sugar before serving.

Recipe 13: Butterbeer

This is everyone's favorite drink. Students and teachers alike look forward to having it on every Hogsmeade visit. Although Harry was never meant to be at Hogsmeade because his permission form was never signed, he managed to get in with the help of the Weasley twins, Fred and George, who gave him the very informative Marauder's Map made for students that are "up to no good" and the help of his very own invisibility cloak which was a Christmas present during his first year. He had the time of his life in Hogsmeade, roaming around Ron and Hermione, although he is partly invisible. The highlight of their visit was a stop at the Three Broomsticks where they ordered a foaming mug of Butterbeer each. Here's the recipe.

Portion Size: 4

Prep Time: 30 Minutes

Ingredient List:

- 4 cups cream soda
- 8 scoops vanilla or butter ice cream
- ¼ cup butterscotch syrup
- Whipped cream for garnish

HHHHHHHHHHHHHHHHHHHHHHHHHHHHHHHHHHHH

How to Cook:

1. Combine all of the ingredients, except for the whipped cream in a blender until smooth. Divide equally into four mugs.

2. Top with whipped cream and serve immediately.

Recipe 14: Melts-in-the-Mouth Choco Pudding

Soon after Harry arrived at Diagon Alley, the Weasleys came by to stay at the Leaky Cauldron together with him. They were coming back from a summer holiday in Egypt where the eldest son Bill was working as a curse breaker for Gringotts. That's where they decided to spend part of Mr. Arthur Weasley's winnings at the annual Galleon Draw sponsored by The Daily Prophet. During their last night at the Leaky Cauldron, the entire family, together with Harry and Hermione, gathered for a scrumptious five-course dinner. This chocolate pudding was what they had for dessert. It's a truly wonderful treat to cap off any meal.

Portion Size: 8

Prep Time: 20 minutes

Ingredient List:

- 1 ¼ cups dark chocolate chips
- 2 tsp. instant coffee powder dissolved in 1 tsp. hot water
- ½ cup brown sugar
- ¼ cup flour
- 4 egg yolks
- 4 whole eggs
- 1 cup butter, divided
- 1 tbsp. chocolate liqueur

For the Chocolate Sauce:

- 1 ¼ cups dark chocolate chips
- 1 cup all-purpose cream

For Garnish:

- Heavy cream
- Honeycomb, coarsely chopped

HHHHHHHHHHHHHHHHHHHHHHHHHHHHHHHHHH

How to Cook:

1. Preheat oven to 350 °F. Grease the 250-millimeter metal molds with melted butter, then arrange them in a baking tray. Set aside.

2. Melt the chocolate chips and butter in a saucepan over low heat, stirring constantly until smooth. Set aside to cool down.

3. Combine the egg yolks, whole eggs, and sugar in a mixing bowl. Continue beating until mixture grew twice as much in size.

4. Fold in the melted chocolate, dissolved coffee, and chocolate liqueur, mixing manually until combined.

5. Add the flour.

6. Spoon batter into prepared molds.

7. Bake for 10 minutes or until the pudding sets.

8. Meanwhile, cook the chocolate sauce by mixing chocolate chips and cream in a saucepan over low heat until smooth or for about 5 minutes.

9. Turn the cooked puddings onto serving plates. Drizzle generously with chocolate sauce. Then, top with heavy cream and chopped honeycomb. Serve.

Recipe 15: Quick and Easy Cheesy Baked Salmon

Harry received an upsetting news the day after his 13th birthday: Aunt Marge (Uncle Vernon's sister, who just like him, enjoys insulting Harry to his face) is coming for a weeklong visit to the Dursleys. Since he has a Hogsmeade form that needs to be signed, Harry promised to follow the story the Dursleys made up about his life, schooling, etc. He got along just fine until the last night when this savory salmon recipe was served. We're sure you did not forget what happened next since Aunt Marge was blown up and all. But there is one more thing we do not want you to forget: this recipe. This quick and easy salmon recipe can be used to please your aunt. Your favorite ones, of course.

Portion Size: 4

Prep Time: 25 Minutes

Ingredient List:

- 2 lbs. salmon fillet, boneless with the skin on
- 2/3 cup cheese, shredded
- Juice of 1 lemon
- 2 cloves garlic, minced
- Cooking spray
- Salt and pepper to taste

For garnish:

- Chopped parsley

How to Cook:

1. Preheat oven to 450 °F.

2. Prepare a baking sheet by lining it with parchment paper and greasing it with some cooking spray.

3. Rub salmon fillets with garlic and place in prepared pan, skin side down.

4. Season the fish with salt and pepper, then drizzle with the lemon juice.

5. Top with cheese.

6. Bake for 15 minutes. Garnish with chopped parsley before serving.

Recipe 16: Pretty Crisp Crumpets

Immediately after Harry arrived at Diagon Alley, the Minister of Magic, Cornelius Fudge, came to somehow shed some light on what would happen to him after blowing up Aunt Marge and leaving the Dursley's home by taking the Knight Bus. He ordered Tom, the innkeeper at the Leaky Cauldron, to set up a private parlor with tea and some crumpets. Crumpets are thick, pancake-like pastries that are best served with afternoon tea. Cooking them takes only about 30 minutes, but you have to rest the batter for a full four hours so you have to mix it in advance.

Portion Size: 6

Prep Time: 30 minutes

Ingredient List:

- 2 2/3 cups flour
- 1 tsp. baking powder
- 1 tsp. yeast
- 2 tsp. salt
- 1 ½ cups milk, warmed
- 1 ½ cups warm water
- 2 tbsp. vegetable oil
- Butter

How to Cook:

1. Mix the flour, yeast, warm water and milk until the batter is runny.

2. Cover the mixing bowl with plastic wrap. Set it aside until the mixture becomes bubbly. This will take about 1-4 hours depending on your room's temperature.

3. Mix in the baking powder and salt.

4. Grease the pan generously with vegetable oil. Heat over medium-low heat, place a crumpet ring into the pan, and fill with the batter just below the top.

5. When bubbles or holes appear, much like in pancakes, turn the crumpets over. Cook until golden brown and crisp on all sides.

6. Serve with butter.

Recipe 17: Cauldron Cakes

The journey toward Hogwarts had been eventful because of the swarming dementors who made Harry pass out. Not to be missed, however, is the plump witch who comes in the middle of the trip with every treat imaginable in a trolley. Harry and his friends, Ron and Hermione, got various goods from the food cart, Cauldron Cakes included. Mind you, these are not only intricately designed but also taste truly wonderful.

Portion Size: 6

Prep Time: 70 minutes

Ingredient List:

- 1 pack Devil's Food Cake mix
- ¾ cup sweetened chocolate chips
- ½ cup marshmallow cream
- ½ cup Confectioner's sugar
- 4 tbsp. butter
- ½ cup vegetable shortening
- 2 tbsp. vanilla extract

For the cauldron handle and feet:

- ½ cup sweetened chocolate chips

How to Cook:

1. Using a metal cupcake mold, bake the devil's food cake mix according to package instructions. Set aside.

2. Meanwhile, prepare chocolate glaze by melting the chocolate chips and butter in a saucepan over low heat, stirring continuously until smooth. Turn off the heat and set aside to cool.

3. To make the marshmallow filling, beat together the prepared marshmallow cream, sugar, vanilla, and shortening until the mixture becomes light and fluffy. Stuff in a pastry bag and set aside.

4. Shape cupcakes into cauldrons, dipping the top into the prepared chocolate glaze and piping marshmallow filling into the cavity. Set aside for the glaze to set.

5. Create the cauldron feet by placing cakes on top of three choco chips arranged in a triangle. Glaze the bottom part to make the chocolate chips stick.

6. For the handle, you will have to melt some chocolate chips, cool them down a little, and then put it in a pastry bag. Pipe a handle shape onto wax paper and let it sit.

7. Once ready, gently attach the handle to the cake. Serve.

Recipe 18: Beauxbatons' Favorite Bouillabaisse

As host to two foreign schools – the Beauxbatons and Durmstrang – for the Triwizard Tournament, Hogwarts' feasts became even more interesting with extraordinary dishes to please the guests' tastes. For the Welcoming Feast held on the 30th of October when the student delegates from abroad came, a French shellfish stew stole the attention of Ron who's used to the usual fare of steak and kidney pie. It would not hurt to open one's penchant for Bouillabaisse, however, as it is definitely a tongue pleaser.

Portion Size: 4

Prep Time: 195 Minutes

Ingredient List:

- 7 oz. salmon fillet, skinned and cubed
- 7 oz. pollock, skinned and cubed
- 7 oz. monkfish, skinned and cubed
- 2 pcs sardine fillets
- 8 pcs mussels, cleaned
- 2 ½ lbs. fish bones
- 1 cup olive oil
- 2 pcs fennel bulbs, chopped
- 2 pcs red peppers, chopped
- 2 ½ lbs. plum tomatoes, chopped
- 1 ½ Tbsp. tomato paste
- 2 ½ Tbsp. tarragon
- 1 tsp. saffron
- Juice of 2 lemons
- 3 tbsp. butter
- Salt and pepper to taste

For the Rouille:

- 3 egg yolks
- 4 garlic cloves, crushed
- 1 cup olive oil
- 1 cup vegetable oil
- Juice of 1 lemon
- Pinch of saffron
- Pinch of cayenne pepper
- Salt and pepper to taste

For Garnishing:

- 1 tsp. basil leaves, chopped
- 1 tsp. tarragon, chopped
- 1 tsp. chives, chopped

HHHHHHHHHHHHHHHHHHHHHHHHHHHHHHHHHHHH

How to Cook:

1. Heat the olive oil in a large saucepan over medium heat.

2. Add the fennel bulbs, stirring continuously for 3 minutes.

3. Whisk in the red peppers and tarragon. Season with salt and pepper. Cook for 2 minutes.

4. Add the tomatoes, tomato paste, fish bones, and saffron. Cover with enough water to simmer for about 90 minutes. Remember to skim off scum.

5. Transfer reduced mixture to a blender to smoothen.

6. Sieve the sauce through a fine mesh, pressing the solids to extract the flavors.

7. Place the sauce back in the blender. Add butter and lemon juice, then bend again. Let the mixture chill.

8. While the mixture is chilling, prepare the Rouille, which is basically a mayo-style sauce. Whisk the egg yolks with saffron, cayenne pepper, and lemon juice. Season with a pinch of salt and pepper.

9. Gradually add the oil and garlic, mixing constantly to your reach your desired thickness.

10. In a large saucepan, stir in the Bouillabaisse sauce and Rouille until well combined. Add chopped monkfish and mussels to cook for 3 minutes.

11. Stir in the pollock and salmon to cook for another 8 minutes.

12. Finally, add the sardines and cook for another minute or two.

13. Spoon stew into a serving bowl. Garnish with tarragon, chives, and basil leaves. Serve warm.

Recipe 19: Sausage Scramble

Harry's summer vacation turned out to be better than the others. He got to spend the rest of it at the Weasley's humble home called The Burrow, joined by Hermione, so they could watch the Quidditch World Cup with the entire family except for its matriarch. Since Mrs. Weasley was not around, you would think that the group would starve in their tent. But no. Mr. Weasley, with the help of the kids, was able to pull off some decent meals, eggs and sausages included. Well, that's the inspiration for this Sausage Scramble recipe. It is definitely worth a try.

Portion Size: 1

Prep Time: 30 Minutes

Ingredient List:

- 1 cup chicken sausage, chopped
- 1 pc egg
- 2 cups boiled potatoes, chopped
- 1 pc green bell pepper, chopped
- 1 pc onion, chopped
- 2 tbsp. parsley, chopped
- 1 Tbsp. virgin olive oil
- Salt and pepper to taste

HHHHHHHHHHHHHHHHHHHHHHHHHHHHHHHHHHHH

How to Cook:

1. Sauté the sausages in heated oil over medium fire, stirring for 3 minutes. Drain on paper towels and set aside.

2. In the same pan, add the onions and bell peppers. Season with salt and pepper, stirring occasionally until tender or for about 5 minutes.

3. Whisk the boiled potatoes into the pan. Cook for a couple of minutes more until the potatoes are completely warmed.

4. Place the sausages back in the pan, mixing well. Adjust the seasoning as needed. Transfer to a serving dish.

5. Cook the egg scramble with a little oil and place it on the sausage platter. Garnish with chopped parsley before serving.

Recipe 20: Holiday Pork Goulash

Christmas is always a favorite time at Hogwarts. Harry, having nowhere else to spend it usually spends it here so he is used to the festivities. But it is different during the fourth year with the Yule Ball happening. Apart from dressing up and being different from their typical selves, there is one thing that remains: the delectable dishes laid out and this pork goulash is part of it.

Portion Size: 4

Prep Time: 50 Minutes

Ingredient List:

- 1 ¼ lbs. pork tenderloin, cut into cubes
- 1 Tbsp. sunflower oil
- 2 tsp. corn flour
- 1 clove garlic, crushed
- 1 pc onion, sliced
- 1 pc red bell pepper, deseeded and chopped
- 8 oz. button mushrooms
- 1 pt. chicken stock
- 1 Tbsp. smoked paprika
- 2 tbsp. tomato purée
- Parsley, chopped

HHHHHHHHHHHHHHHHHHHHHHHHHHHHHHHHHHHH

How to Cook:

1. Brown the pork pieces in a greased pan over high heat. Transfer into a bowl. Set aside.

2. Using the same pan, sauté the garlic and onion in oil until the onions become translucent.

3. Add paprika, stirring for a minute before adding the stock.

4. Bring the mixture to a boil, then whisk in the tomato puree and browned pork.

5. Reduce the heat to medium and simmer for 15 minutes.

6. Add the mushrooms and red bell peppers and continue to cook for another 10 minutes.

7. Meanwhile, make a smooth paste by dissolving corn flour in cold water.

8. Stir in the corn flour mixture to the goulash, mixing until the sauce thickens.

9. Garnish with chopped parsley before serving.

Recipe 21: Hagrid's No-Fail Beef Casserole

Harry, Ron, and Hermione know better than to trust Hagrid's cooking, but they can never escape it since they are almost always around the gamekeeper's hut. Just like the day after the foreign students came. They came down to see Hagrid and asked him what he knew about the tournament. In the course of their conversation, they end up having lunch with their big friend. Expectedly, they did not really appreciate the dish, especially after Hermione scooped talon leaves out of her meal. But we promise you will enjoy this beef casserole version which is definitely free of talon leaves.

Portion Size: 4

Prep Time: 100 minutes

Ingredient List:

- 2 lbs. beef, cut into cubes
- 8 pcs onions, peeled and halved
- 2 cups baby potatoes
- 2 pcs carrots, sliced
- 1 cup small button mushrooms
- 1 Tbsp. flour
- 1 Tbsp. olive oil
- 2 tbsp. tomato paste
- 1 cup beef stock
- 1 cup red wine
- 1 pc bay leaf
- Salt and pepper to taste
- Thyme sprigs
- 2 tbsp. parsley, roughly chopped

HHHHHHHHHHHHHHHHHHHHHHHHHHHHHHHHHHHHH

How to Cook:

1. Preheat oven to 375 °F.

2. Coat beef cubes in flour.

3. Brown beef in oil over high heat. Stir in the sliced carrots and onion halves. Stir constantly until cooked through and browned.

4. Stir in the tomato paste, beef stock, wine, bay leaf, and thyme. Season with salt and pepper to taste, stirring to combine, and bringing to a boil.

5. Cover dish and bake for 60 minutes.

6. After the first hour, add the mushrooms and potatoes, then continue to bake for another half an hour until the beef cubes are soft and flavorful.

7. Sprinkle with chopped parsley before serving.

Recipe 22: Pale Blancmange

This not-so-pretty dessert, at least in the eyes of Hogwarts students who are used to the extravagance of eloquent puddings and tarts, is actually not bad at all. Served at the welcome dinner that officially opened the Triwizard Tournament, Blancmange is a rich and flavorful treat that washes down the meats and all the grease that came with the night's roasts.

Portion Size: 6

Prep Time: 60 Minutes

Ingredient List:

- 2 tbsp. sugar
- 2 cups milk
- 2 tbsp. corn flour
- 1 tsp. vanilla

HHHHHHHHHHHHHHHHHHHHHHHHHHHHHHHHHHHHH

How to Cook:

1. Combine the sugar and milk in a heavy-bottomed saucepan. Heat over medium-low heat until it comes to a soft boil.

2. Turn off the heat before adding the corn flour. Stir continuously until the mixture becomes smooth.

3. Place the pan back onto the stove heating until it boils. Add vanilla, stirring until well combined.

4. Transfer mixture to the desired mold and set aside in the fridge to cool completely.

Recipe 23: Delightful Breakfast Toast

One of the things that Harry faced in this fifth book is the persecution from the Ministry of Magic about underage magic. You see, underage wizards are not allowed to perform magic outside of Hogwarts, which Harry did, specifically to conjure a Patronus because the Dementors endangered his life and Dudley's life. On the day of his hearing, Mrs. Weasley offered him everything for breakfast, but he refused and just settled with some toast, which he even had a hard time swallowing. If your toast recipe is as good as this, however, you will never have to worry about not being hungry.

Portion Size: 6

Prep Time: 25 minutes

Ingredient List:

- 12 slices white bread
- 4 tsp. butter
- 4 eggs
- ½ cup half &half
- ½ tsp. salt
- 2 tsp. sugar
- ½ tsp. vanilla
- ¼ tsp. cinnamon powder
- 1 Tbsp. sugar

HHHHHHHHHHHHHHHHHHHHHHHHHHHHHHHHHHHHHH

How to Cook:

1. Preheat oven to 425 °F. Grease the baking dish with melted butter. Set aside.

2. Lightly beat the eggs, then add cream, salt, sugar, vanilla extract, and cinnamon powder.

3. Allow the bread to soak into mixture until fully coated. Transfer onto prepared baking sheet.

4. Bake for 10 minutes or until golden brown.

5. Sprinkle with powdered sugar before serving.

Recipe 24: Steak and Kidney Pie

For the welcome feast, Hogwarts was its festive self once again. All the four house tables – Gryffindor, Hufflepuff, Ravenclaw, and Slytherin – were filled with delectable recipes you could ever imagine. Among the regular fare is this Steak and Kidney Pie.

Portion Size: 8

Prep Time: 30 minutes

Ingredient List:

- 1 lb. chuck steak, finely chopped
- 2 pcs lamb kidneys, finely chopped
- ½ cup red wine
- ½ tsp. cayenne pepper
- ¼ tsp. salt

For the Dough:

- 2 ½ cups all-purpose flour
- 1/3 cup water
- 1 cup unsalted butter, chilled
- 2 tbsp. melted butter for brushing pies

HHHHHHHHHHHHHHHHHHHHHHHHHHHHHHHHHHH

How to Cook:

1. Preheat oven to 400 °F.

2. Grease the muffin trays with cooking spray. Set aside.

3. Make the dough by mixing flour, salt, and butter continuously until you have coarse dough.

4. Gradually add water while mixing to get the dough consistency you need.

5. Divide dough equally in two, then, roll out each portion into 1/8-inch thick sheets.

6. Use the first sheet for the pastry base and the other one for the cover. Cut circles on them using a glass rim or cookie cutter.

7. Gently lay down pastry base on muffin tins, then, set aside.

8. Combine the meats, cayenne pepper, and salt in a bowl.

9. Scoop a spoonful of the mixture into the dough-lined muffin tins. Drizzle with red wine before placing the top on and sealing the edges.

10. Brush the top with melted butter. Then, bake for 30-40 minutes.

Recipe 25: Pumpkin Pasties

The trolley treats are difficult to turn down, even in light of the grief that Harry has been nursing in his heart for the death of Sirius, his long-lost godfather. Although, not the usual giddy students, Harry and his friends tried to look to the future with hope, enjoying some Pumpkin Pasties on their journey back to King's Cross Station after the term. Intrigued about what they are like? Don't be. We have got the recipe here.

Portion Size: 8

Prep Time: 75 minutes

Ingredient List:

- 1 32-oz package pie crust
- 1 cup mashed potato
- 1 lb. pumpkin, pureed
- ½ cup cheese, shredded
- 6 pcs bacon, browned and crumbled
- 1 tsp. mustard powder
- egg wash
- Salt and pepper to taste

HHHHHHHHHHHHHHHHHHHHHHHHHHHHHHHHHHHHHHH

How to Cook:

1. Preheat your oven to 350 °F.

2. Meanwhile, line a baking dish with parchment paper. Set aside.

3. Combine the pumpkin puree, mashed potato, cheese, bacon, and mustard powder.

4. Season to taste with salt and pepper. Set aside.

5. Roll the pastry dough into 1/8-inch sheet, dividing equally into 8.

6. Spoon the pumpkin filling onto each of the pastry dough, sealing the edges with a fork.

7. Brush the pasties with an egg wash and cut slits into the top before baking until golden brown, about 50 minutes or more.

Recipe 26: English Porridge

Porridge is often a game-changer at Hogwarts breakfasts. It was mentioned several times, specifically in Chapter Nine of The Half-Blood Prince. Try this recipe and you will understand why Harry, Ron, and Hermione can't turn down an offer for this delightful and filling treat.

Portion Size: 2

Prep Time: 20 Minutes

Ingredient List:

- ½ cup steel-cut oats
- ½ cup rolled oats
- 2 cups whole milk, divided
- 1 ½ cups water
- 1 ½ tsp. sea salt
- 2 tbsp. maple syrup

How to Cook:

1. Combine the milk, water, and salt in a pot. Boil over medium heat.

2. Add in the oats, stirring occasionally until done, about 15 minutes.

3. Serve in separate bowls, make a well in the middle, and add a tbsp. of maple syrup to each serving.

Recipe 27: Slughorn's Crystallized Pineapples

One of the most crucial and memorable parts in the sixth Harry installment is how the retired Professor Slughorn is convinced to come back and teach at Hogwarts. Albus Dumbledore relayed several thoughts he remembers about the professor to Harry. Slughorn's love of crystallized pineapples was one of them. This is among the simplest yet tastiest recipes you could find in this cookbook.

Portion Size: 10

Prep Time: 50 Minutes

Ingredient List:

- 20 pcs pineapple slices, reserve heavy syrup
- ¼ cup corn syrup
- 3 cups sugar, divided

HHHHHHHHHHHHHHHHHHHHHHHHHHHHHHHHHHHHHH

How to Cook:

1. In a saucepan over medium heat, dissolve 2 ½ cups sugar in heavy pineapples syrup and corn syrup, stirring frequently until the mixture comes to a boil, about 4-5 minutes.

2. Reduce the heat before adding pineapples, coating both sides with the mixture.

3. Allow the pineapples to cook until they are translucent, about 45 minutes.

4. Arrange on a wire rack to dry overnight.

Recipe 28: Roast Chicken Legs and Chips

Harry missed the welcome feast at the Great Hall another time and this time it was because of Draco Malfoy. Hungry and covered in blood, he gladly reached out for chicken legs and chips on the table, only to find them disappearing before he could even take a bite. Curious about what they must be like? We duplicated that recipe here.

Portion Size: 4

Prep Time: 80 minutes

Ingredient List:

- 8 pcs chicken legs
- 2 lbs. potatoes, cut into thick wedges, skin on
- 3 tbsp. olive oil
- 1 pc chicken bouillon, crushed
- 1 tsp. smoked paprika
- 2 tbsp. sea salt
- 1 cup Kiev butter

How to Cook:

1. Preheat oven to 425 °F.

2. Arrange the chicken legs on a wire rack over a roasting tin. Spread with Kiev butter, then sprinkle with the salt, crumbled chicken bouillon, and paprika.

3. Meanwhile, boil potatoes for 5 minutes, drain, and set aside to cool.

4. Place the olive oil in a baking pan and heat on the oven. Add the potatoes in hot oil, season with the remaining salt, chicken bouillon, and paprika, turning a couple of times to coat.

5. Roast chicken for about 20 minutes, with the potatoes baking tray at the bottom.

6. Turn the chicken legs over to brown the other side after 20 minutes. Cook for another 25 minutes until both chicken and potatoes are cooked and nicely brown.

Recipe 29: Hagrid's Rock Cakes

It was the first time Harry, Ron, and Hermione had a heated argument with Hagrid. It was because the three friends decided that it was in their best interest not to enlist in the Care of Magical Creatures' NEWT. Although huge and grumpy, Hagrid cannot stay mad at the three, managing to serve them a plate of rock cakes and brown tea. Hungry, Harry reached over for the food, although he never really liked the surprises in Hagrid's cooking. This recipe does not have such a surprise and will amaze you with the delicious flavors.

Portion Size: 6

Prep Time: 35 Minutes

Ingredient List:

- 2 cups flour
- ½ tsp. salt
- 1 tsp. baking soda
- 1/3 cup sugar
- 1/3 cup raisins
- ½ cup butter, chilled
- 2 tbsp. milk
- 1 tsp. vanilla
- 1 pc egg
- Coarse sugar for garnish

HHHHHHHHHHHHHHHHHHHHHHHHHHHHHHHHHHHH

How to Cook:

1. Preheat your oven to 400 °F.

2. Line a large baking tray with parchment paper and set aside.

3. Lightly beat the egg together with water and vanilla in a bowl. Set aside.

4. In a mixing bowl, whisk the flour, baking soda, and salt. Cut in the butter and continue to mix until crumbly.

5. Stir in the sugar and then the raisins.

6. Add the egg mixture, stirring until all the ingredients come together.

7. Scoop a tbsp. of batter, making a ball, then coat with sugar before arranging onto prepared baking tray.

8. Bake for 12 minutes or more, until the cakes are a nice golden color.

Recipe 30: Wild Mushrooms Dinner

As Harry, Ron, and Hermione set off into the wild, they barely had something decent to eat. Hermione, having packed all the essentials in her bewitched beady bag but forgot to pack food, was reduced to looking for wild mushrooms and cooking them in a can. We made sure, however, that you are not going to brood as Ron did because this wild mushroom recipe is delectable indeed.

Portion Size: 4

Prep Time: 17 minutes

Ingredient List:

- 6 cups mixed mushrooms, sliced
- 1 Tbsp. fresh thyme, roughly chopped
- 2 tsp. olive oil
- 2 garlic cloves, minced
- Salt and pepper to taste

HHHHHHHHHHHHHHHHHHHHHHHHHHHHHHHHHHHHH

How to Cook:

1. Sauté the garlic in a skillet with olive oil over medium heat.

2. Add the mushrooms, stirring occasionally to cook through, about 3-5 minutes.

3. Stir in the thyme, then season with salt and pepper, and serve.

Recipe 31: Kreacher's French Onion Soup

Kreacher had always been a reluctant house elf who was left Harry's care when his godfather died and decided to give him all his possessions. The air changed; however, when Harry handed Kreacher a duplicate locket that once belonged to the latter's favorite master, Sirius's brother Regulus. This French Onion Soup is one of the surprisingly amazing offers Kreacher gave his master.

Portion Size: 2

Prep Time: 30 Minutes

Ingredient List:

- 2 pcs onions, sliced into strips
- 1 Tbsp. flour
- 1 Tbsp. butter
- ¼ cup red wine
- 2 ½ cups beef stock
- 1 tsp. thyme
- Bay leaf
- Salt, pepper, and sugar to taste
- French baguette slices with butter and Parmesan cheese

HHHHHHHHHHHHHHHHHHHHHHHHHHHHHHHHHHHH

How to Cook:

1. Sauté the onions in a medium saucepan with melted butter. Stir frequently until the onion slices become translucent.

2. Season the onions with sugar, salt, and freshly ground pepper, cooking for some minutes more until they turn brown.

3. Add the flour, red wine, and stock, stirring until smooth.

4. Whisk in the thyme and bay leaf. Then, bring the soup to a nice simmer for half an hour.

5. Top with buttery cheese baguettes before serving.

Recipe 32: Cheesy Garlic Pull Apart Bread

Harry's return to the Hogwarts grounds with Ron and Hermione was met with swarming Death Eaters and Dementors alike. Good thing, Albus Dumbledore's brother, Aberforth, was there to cover for them. He not only saved their necks but also served their hungry spirits a delightful serving of bread, cheese, and mead. Since we thought that simple loaf and cheese slices were a bit mediocre, we decided to make this bread recipe that deliciously pulls apart with creamy cheese. After all, this one is the last of the meals mentioned in the book since the rest was dedicated to the fighting and more fighting to put the wizarding community right again.

Portion Size: 8

Prep Time: 30 Minutes

Ingredient List:

- 1 pc sourdough
- ¾ cup Mozzarella cheese, shredded
- 2/3 cup butter, melted
- 2 tbsp. minced garlic
- 1 Tbsp. parsley, finely chopped
- Salt to taste

How to Cook:

1. Preheat oven to 350 °F.

2. Combine the butter, garlic, and parsley. Heat in the microwave oven and set aside.

3. Create diagonal slits in the sourdough, making sure that you do not cut through.

4. Pry open the slits, stuff cheese and garlic butter into the slits in the bread.

5. Cover the bread in aluminum foil and bake for 15 minutes.

6. Peel off the foil and continue baking for 5 minutes more until bread is crusty and golden brown.

Recipe 33: Artichoke Canapés

With a plan to take down the Dark Lord together with Ron and Hermione, Harry would love as much to be alone planning. However, Mrs. Weasley tried to keep them away, frightened of what they might decide to do in the coming days. That's why she kept them busy doing different things to keep them away. While he and Ron were assigned to cleaning tasks and degnoming the garden, Hermione was left to help in the kitchen. Canapés are just some of the amazing dishes they prepared for the upcoming wedding of Bill and Fleur.

Portion Size: 6

Prep Time: 30 Minutes

Ingredient List:

- 1 lb. puff pastry, thawed
- 1 8-oz bottle artichoke hearts
- 1 cup feta cheese, crumbled
- 1 pc egg, lightly beaten
- 4 tbsp. thyme leaves, coarsely chopped

HHHHHHHHHHHHHHHHHHHHHHHHHHHHHHHHHHHHH

How to Cook:

1. Preheat oven to 450 °F.

2. Grease a baking sheet with some cooking spray and set aside.

3. Roll out the thawed pastry sheet into 1/8-inch thickness. Cut into bite-size squares.

4. Brush puff pastry with egg, then top them with the artichoke, cheese, and thyme leaves.

5. Bake for 10 minutes.

Author's Afterthoughts

THANK YOU

You will not regret your choice to buy my book and read it from beginning to end! Thank you for taking precious time out of your day to peruse my work and try a recipe or two. My hope is that you find benefit within its pages and your culinary skills progress beyond the content.

There is an overwhelming variety of choices in the world today, so the fact that you considered your options and decided to take a chance on my work fills me with gratitude.

Fill in an online review on Amazon and let me know what you thought! Don't hold back, I want your honest opinion. Others will benefit from your experience and I will get the necessary feedback I need to create better books in the future!

Thank you,

Meg Blair

Printed in Great Britain
by Amazon